TO SIGH

To Sigh was written in May of 2019 while a 3Arts Fellow at the MacDowell Colony.

Printed in the United States of America

First Printing, Hardback 2020
Paperback 2023

Hardback ISBN: 978-1-7347545-0-6
Paperback ISBN: 978-1-955498-03-6

Press Here
410 S Michigan Ave Suite 420
Chicago, IL 60605

mattbodett.com
pressherestudio.com

The Art Institute of Chicago received a gift of artworks from the Edlis Neeson Collection. Among them was a painting,

"Untitled (1969)"

by Cy Twombly.

The following is a guide to reading that painting.

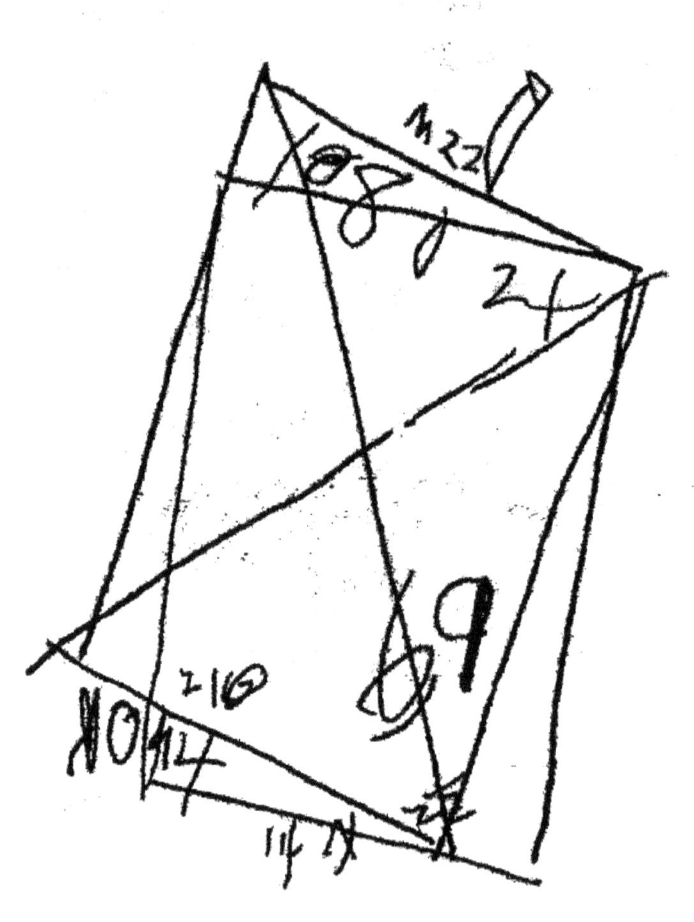

If it went to boxed and collected
the same the way to
1081
Returns
Returns
Casual nonchalance,
not like caring year seems length
Possessive and control
Form
In winded on winded
One
Name
Place
Science
Countered
Do you seem balance
or year or position
Stained or claimed
to be the same time
Name name
Encounter the diatribe
it seems like the specimen
is well cared for, you've placed it and
tagged it and numbered
it and sampled it and placed
it and placed for it to
Crash seem breath
And caged in negation
Casual rust is different than neglect

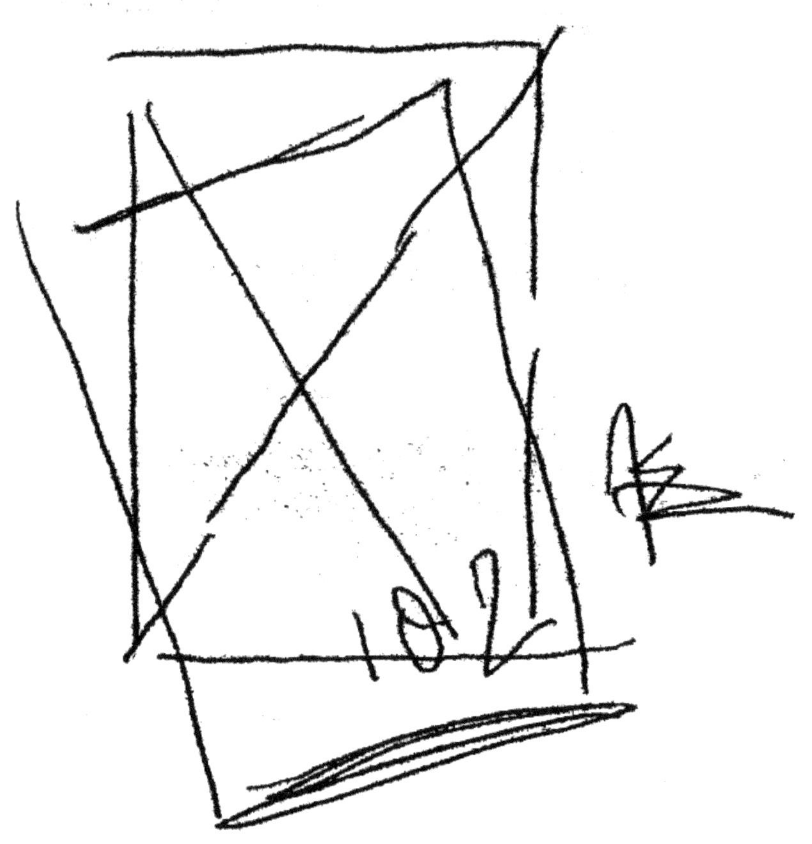

The specimen is well cared for you've
placed it
and tagged it and numbered
it and sampled it and placed
it and placed for it to
Strike
And for the way to
seem like the breathing
was not just casual
the way the sky is letting go of the
Methods of trying to care
And fleeting
the sound is not numbered
Like the
shoelaces and the knots
and the nots and the cannots
Skipping dust
and forming the absence
And free to care like rust
Measure
It is length
And scale
And rustle
And position the wind in the sails
You seem to negate
Castle
Bricked and stoned and baulked
cringe when the dagger pierces flesh
It isn't about crying

hr
th
sndt
l
w

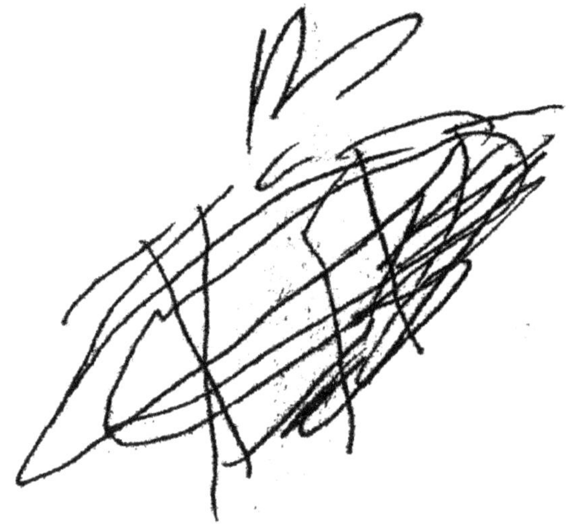

And doubt and pierce
And Didymus
Forming the side and the scale of the
wound and open
gape and for the caring there isn't
a place to stop the
hollow stick of sounding the pass
And when form
And
put your finger here;
see my hands,
stop doubting and believe
flesh and wide skies and feeling
belonging
To seem
like the way to soften the notion and
classed to the scale
Of the crushing thorn
As weight
It lights
Teeth
As biting and mouthed and gripped
Whose flesh

fst
lr
m
m
ott

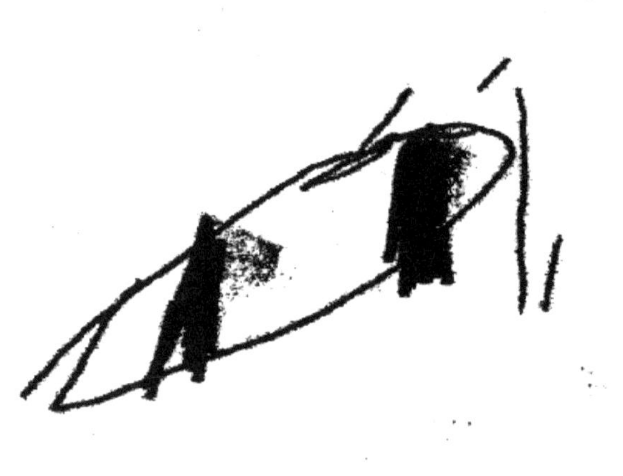

Boated and rafted
Board
Boarded
Boarding
Crushing the sparrow weight and
The specimen of a bird
The dead
The weight
Of the specimen
Of the bird boarded
Of the boat of the bird
And passing into the cast with form
Or strapped
Or jacketed to the
Straight
With buckles
not showing and cowered to crawl
The floor of deck
And salt
And waxed to keep its shine
And do it flight winded to seem faster
In lite
It's is like your name

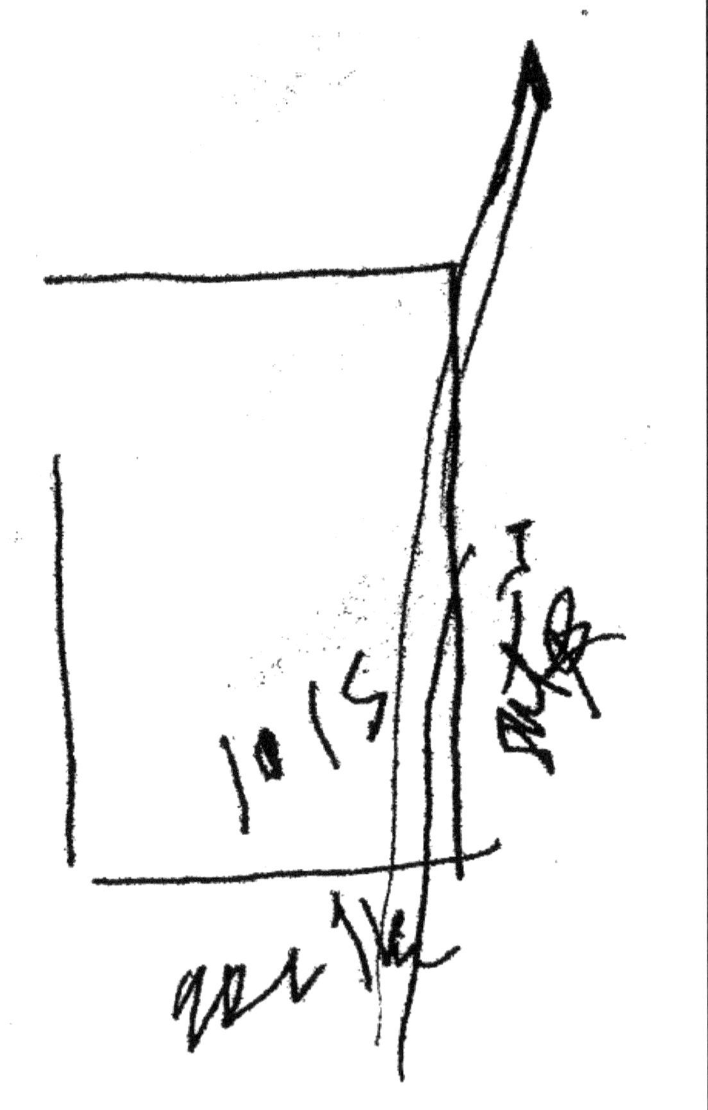

Home is little step
With path and speaking
Curling the trauma
Or the indulgence
When does
the time right sort to the way
the baskets produce the goods
To become like the
intimacy of your place
Can't say
And won't
Like slipping the mud
Like slipping the
Not casua
Not supposed to say the dropp
On the sounded like
Directions cause the raining
Damage
To seem the
Frame to
Secured name
Length
To hold to
Delineate
Demarcate
De
Destr
D
Why are you crying

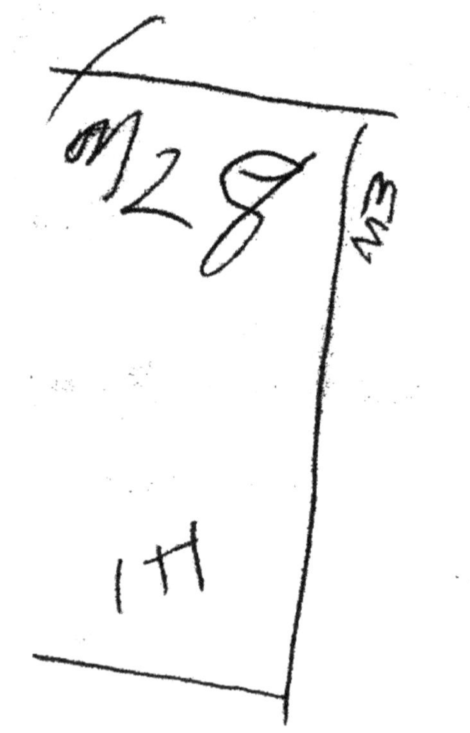

Mine is like the way to age
The way to see the methods of
Numerous crimes and
Not simple
As a way of knowing the casual
The age
The weight
The salted seeing
The edge of what a place
To become
There was a lake
at the edge but know body knew
How to retrieve the boat
Its
With casual
Crushing
I saw a wild turkey pass this way
Across the range of dead grass
Or living
Or boat
It is a passage
A right way to pass
and a right way to possess
Can you settle the name
How many days

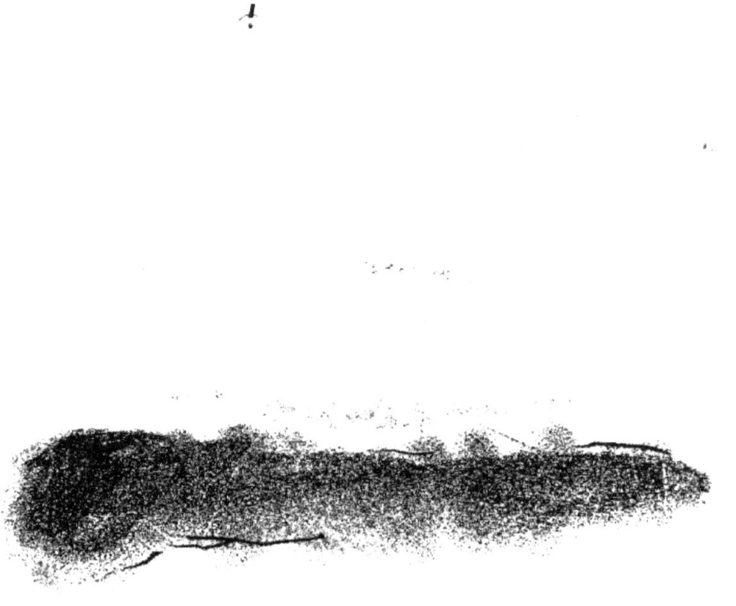

Cannon
It was on the edge of the lake
If memory serves me correctly
It can pass
It can't solve the
Washing the salt from the wound
Is it healing?
Or flaccid dreaming
Elongated fleshy
Not
Is aside
Don't drown
The way to see smiling
And ash

ss
rt
fr
mt!
10

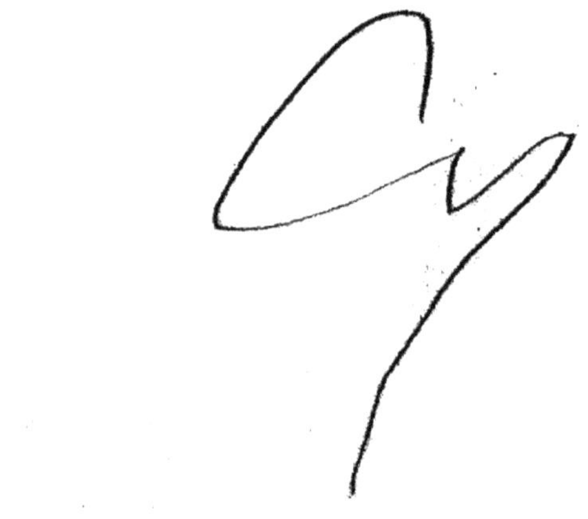

Out breathing
Named like the
Movement to flow and ebb
A shadow moves the same as a cloud
It isn't like dying

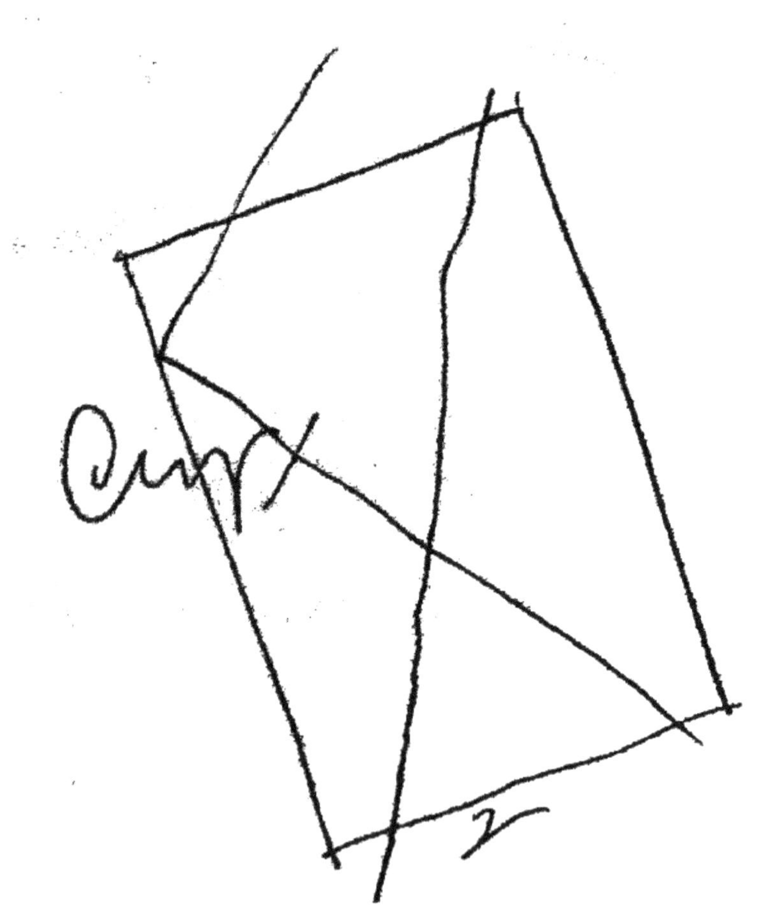

Simple
To thinking and decaying
And when it's the way
to sound a word at the end of a breath
And the exhale
And when does the word actually end
Is it the last part of the breath
Or the last part of the weight
Last part of thought
And when you lose a shadow
It's the end of the position
To move
The climb
The way a blanket covers or
The canceled plate prints
Or the do you make a sound
When the brand hits the flesh
That is the question
And noble seems out of line
At this point
And decay
It is a way to cheer

ftt
plc
ssnt
ccl
prrt
fts
stl
ttm

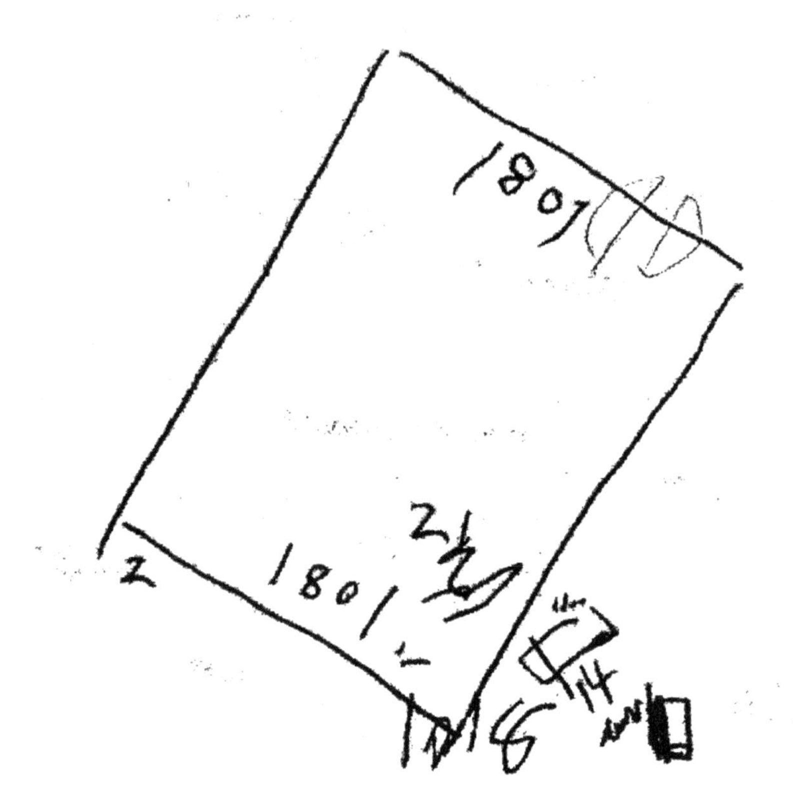
1801
1801
2
6
14

It is an American yacht
Or the year
Or the way a vice
Stumped
And is that the length
Of caring
A breach of shore
Set aside the fallow fleshy
What is blue
It stands
It waves or washes
I wish I knew
And canceled
It was like a system
And when it was a
system it numbered and
The specimen was well cared for and
placed and tagged and numbered and
sampled and
placed and placed for it to
What is the size
Of shore
Or breach
Or care
Can it contain
And wash
It's a quilt
Your name is on the lower corner
in wax

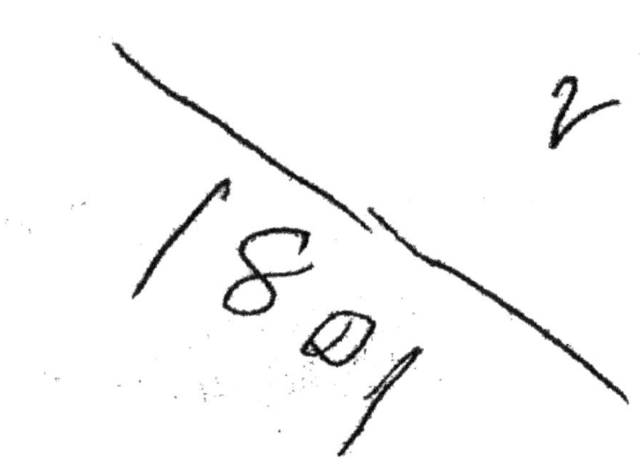

Two halves and
consider who was appointed
John Marshall
And born
Brigham Young
What is your history
To solemn
To fear
Or is it confide and
Wrap
And
When it is too simple
it cries in the dark
Like blocks
Of salt on the way to
Licking wounds or
Sounded like
A weight
And a bird shored on the thorn
Put your finger here
Your nose on the spot
Your doubt in the way of finding

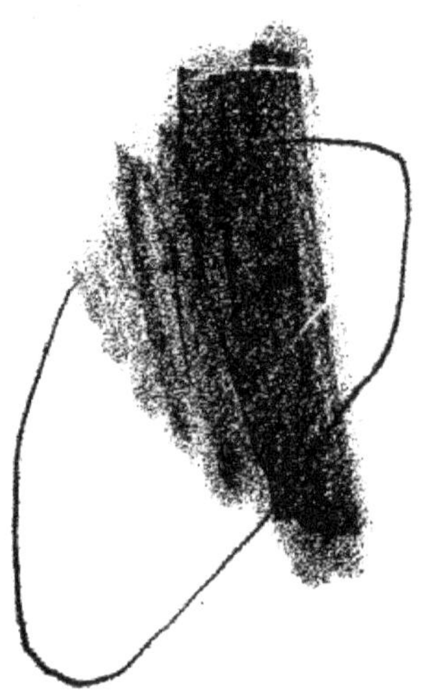

In a reflection of
Sees the way you can disappear
The way a
name sinks into the shape of
Faces and nomenclature
And who knew the definition to that
When the sinking swallowed
The way a word ends on a breath
The way a sound carries
Is it more like the casting of lots
Or the carrying of weighted wood
In ships on boats in rafts on mind
In felled
Forrests whisper
Names to seem like songs
Sixty nine feet
Or July
Or when
Found the way a whisper catches

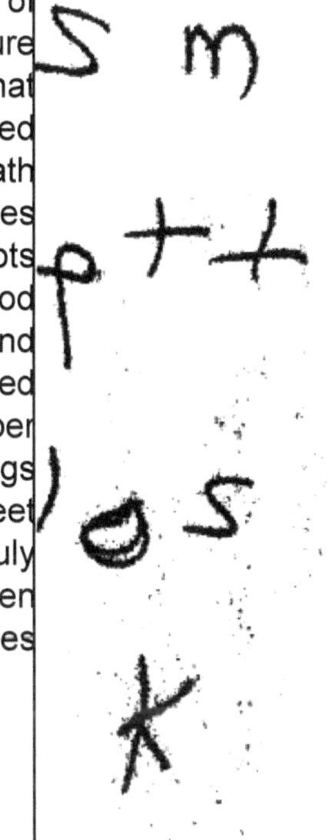

Sixty nine ways to
Two
Eleven or sounds like oven
Or sounds like
Who could
Sound the
When you face
the direction of the wound
Its easier to finger the gap of belief
Sigh the non
To sing the way to
those who always believed
To have always doubted
That's in a name
Marked off
Square
Canceled with the way time slinks
Do you hear the way it settles?
I can't make my feet any heavier

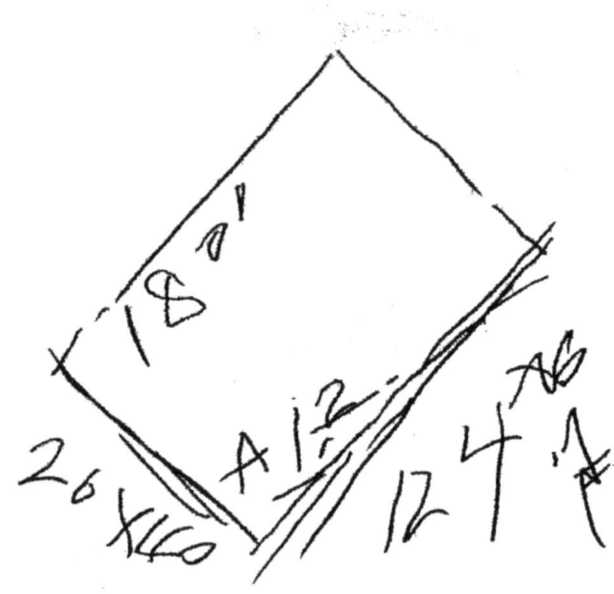

Framed and
Incised
Whose got the right length of spirit
And when I wallow in
A
Single age
Twice
I single the same tepid
Rice
And Lillies rise to meet
The surface
In the mud
weight settles and feeds
Yours is not the numbered system
The method of measuring
The way to sailing
To seem like a crash
A wreck
You need to find a shore

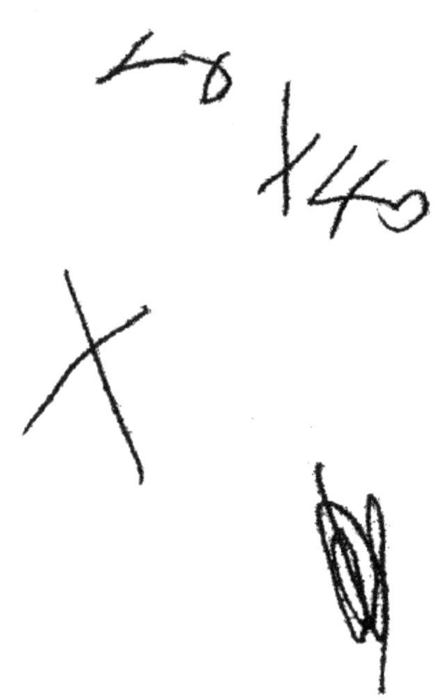

Something like a map
Or not a map
Like a writing desk
Can answer all belonging
To a bird
Then swallows the weight of sinking
Or marked
Or what does neutral mean
Did you know that they used to sing
All out loud
Here
And the gravel remembers their tone

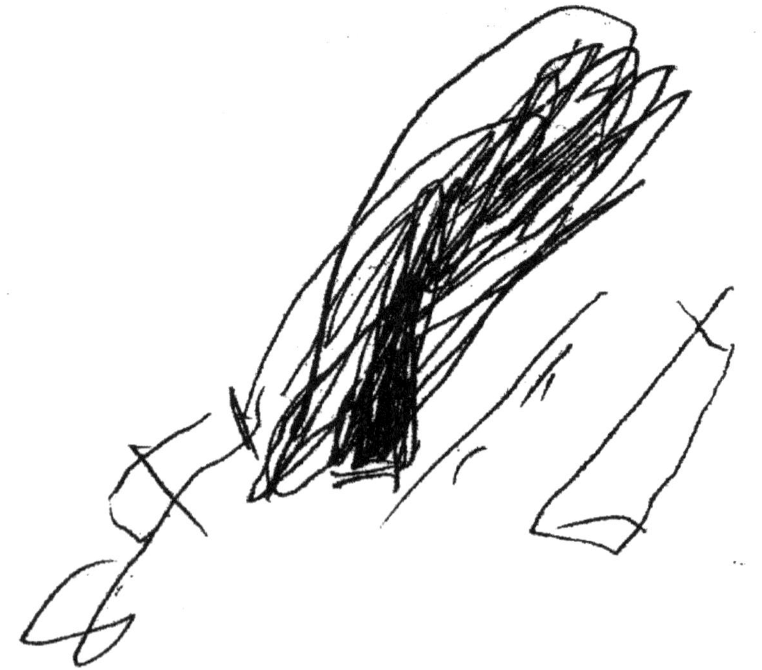

It isn't like pain
Like forgetting to pain
Like slowly bringing forgetting
Its a picture
A single mark or Thomas
When you wander the
desert do you sing?
Drop
Dropp
Flooded to single
It broke the levee and drowned the
You knew their names
And they still
Becoming the sound of breath to sing
When does it end?
And the end of the sound?
I do not
understand your
decision to cancel your plan
You assume plan

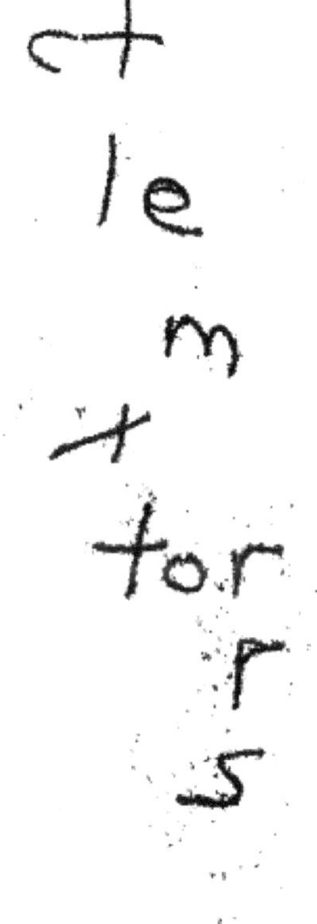

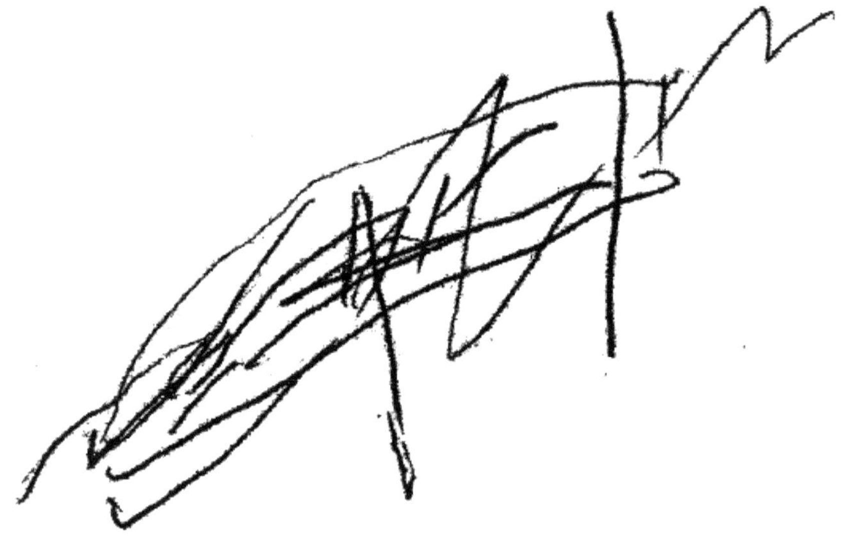

Is it greed to assume that
To wind
It was simply the way to block out the
They are connected
Roped together like a raft
cinched at the waist
Or crushed
It was under foot
A print
A way to see the weight
Like they traveled and moved
Into the rain
And it was covered up
In mud and
Washed in the way to remain
Simply to touch the
West wind and sail
Its about the salt in the air
Fellow
I can't be sure
about how to care
about the way to
make the way to be
the same as the
way to the signal for help
Its about the smoke and not the fire

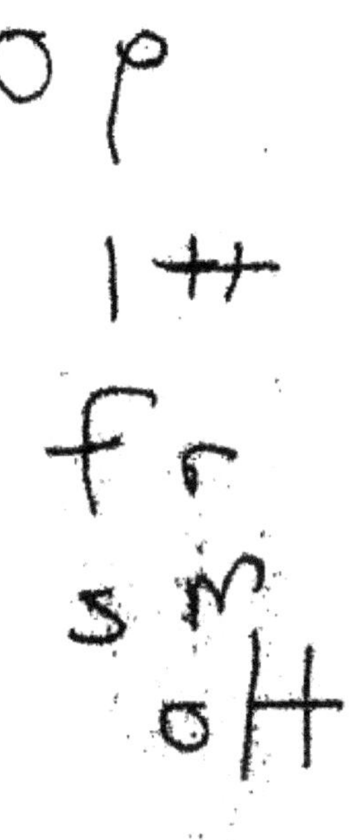

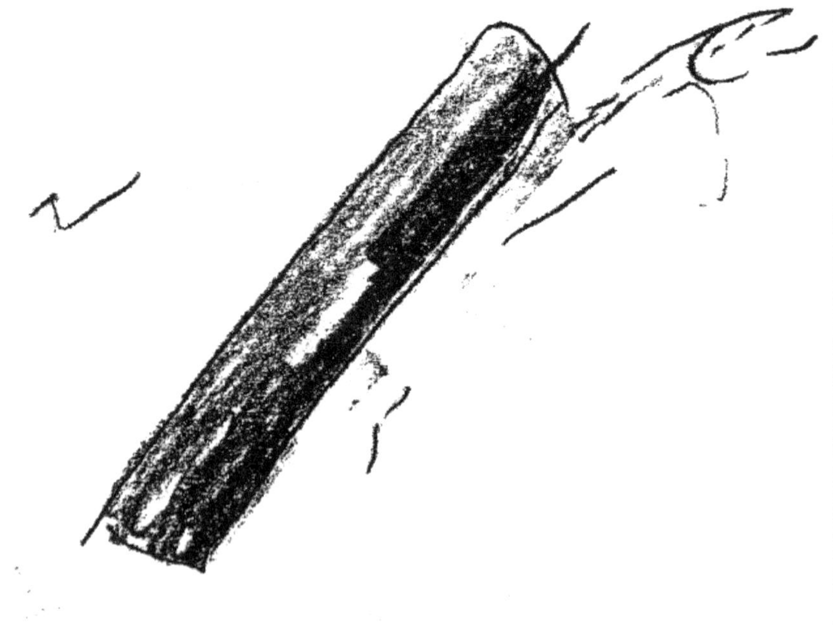

Bar
Refrain
Rest
Cast
Length
Iron
Road
Stud
Beam
Pole
Rod
Strike
Bellow
Pummel
When it is crushed
it is the sound releasing

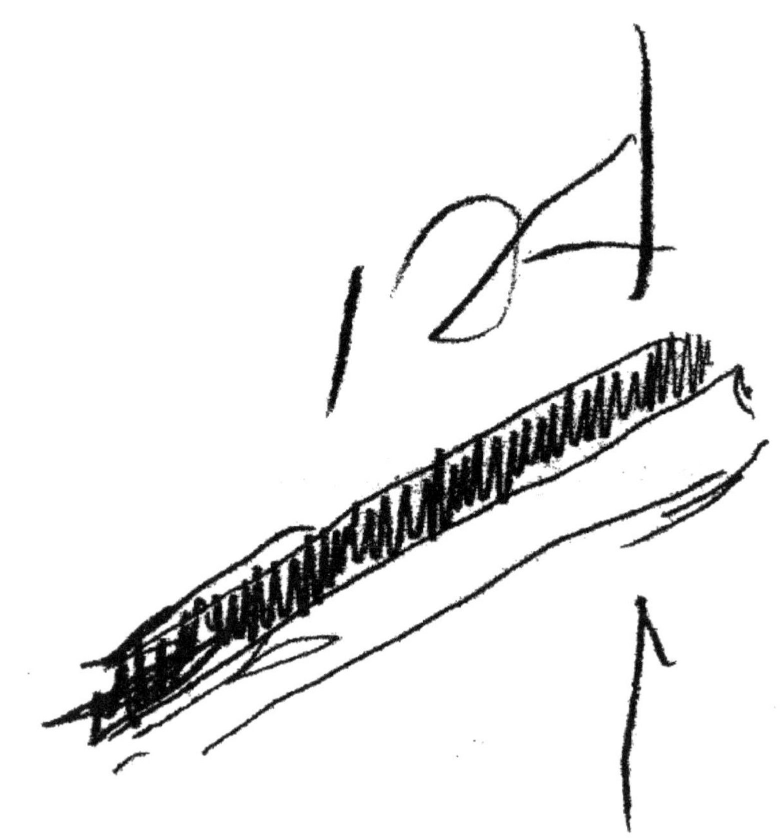

Something like a landscape
On a beach
It is the wooded faint smell
Dust in the throat
Its a dry day to be so thirsty
When the wind is patterned
It is because of the length
Of the boat
Or the birds singing path
To here
And lost in the method of numbering
seemed to have
created a specimen to care for
Cannot spell name
And name
And finally

b n o
th

m
llo
st

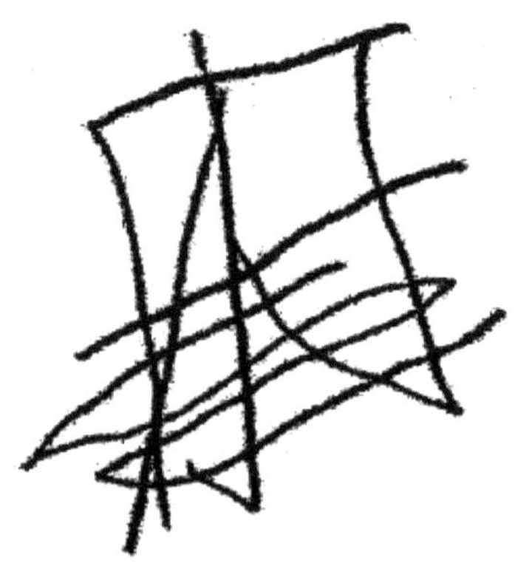

It isn't about migration is it?
Not tied up in fancy
And wrestling with fleeting
Or remembering
It was a way to support your ambition
It was a way to supplant ecologies
I marked it on the
Way to seem like
such a simple method
It was rowing out to the boat
The shore was a distance
And it is length
When time and
what was the name for memory
And fog
Or little ways of seeing home
Or little sticks that resemble
It is quaint
A knick knack
Water sinks in the bathtub
Just like weight and time

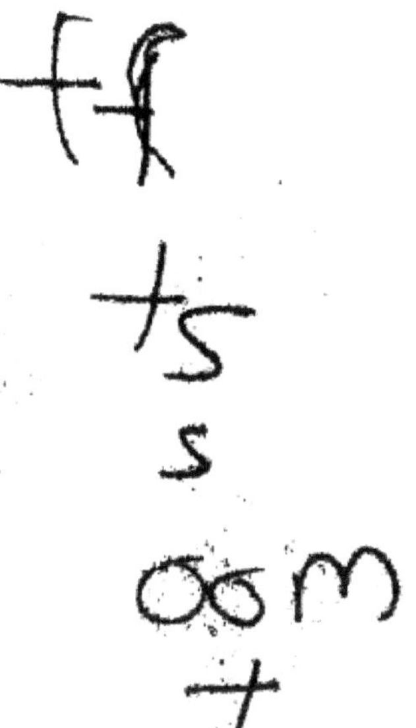

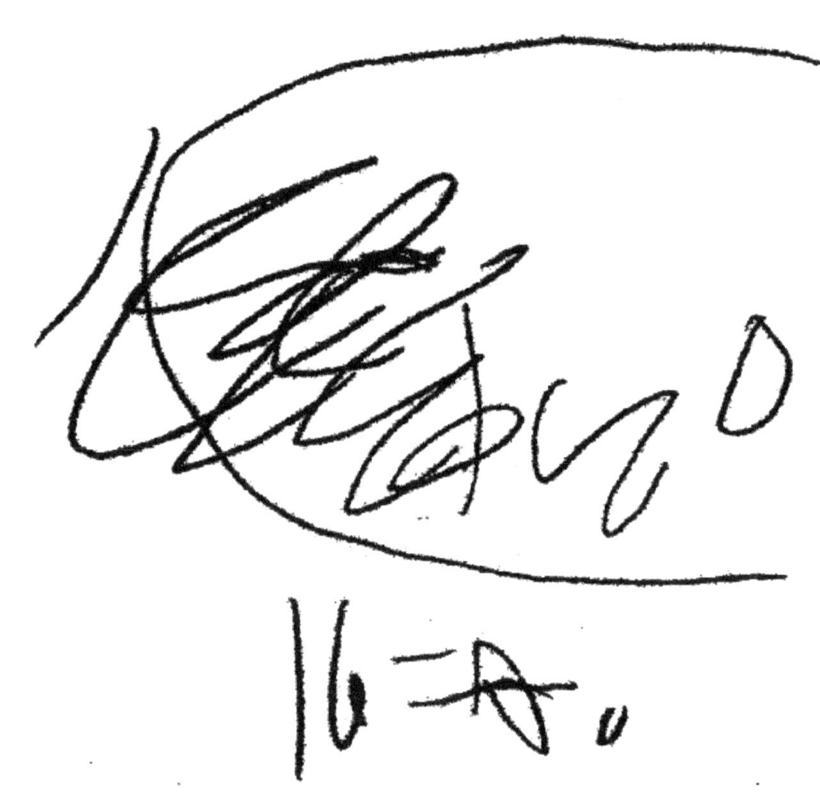

Funny
How you were trying to capture
The method
Of capturing the
Method
The winds or the ways to star the
Shore
And rain
And capture the sounding
Way to capture
The sighing way to see the
Specimen was carefully considered
And numbered and
placed and placed for it to
When did you start collecting
Caring to sort the
It was nonsense really
Nobody noticed
the sound of not caring
Or safety
Circled by
An indication only

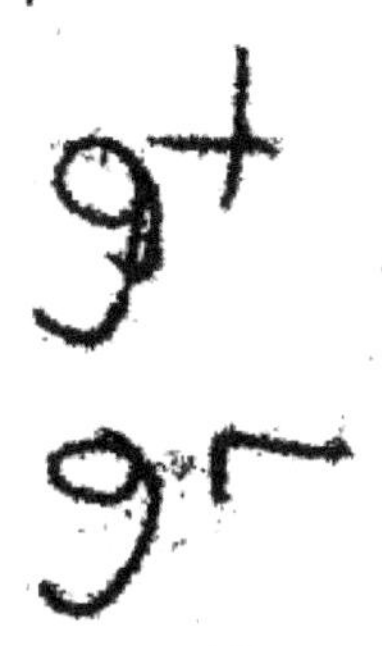

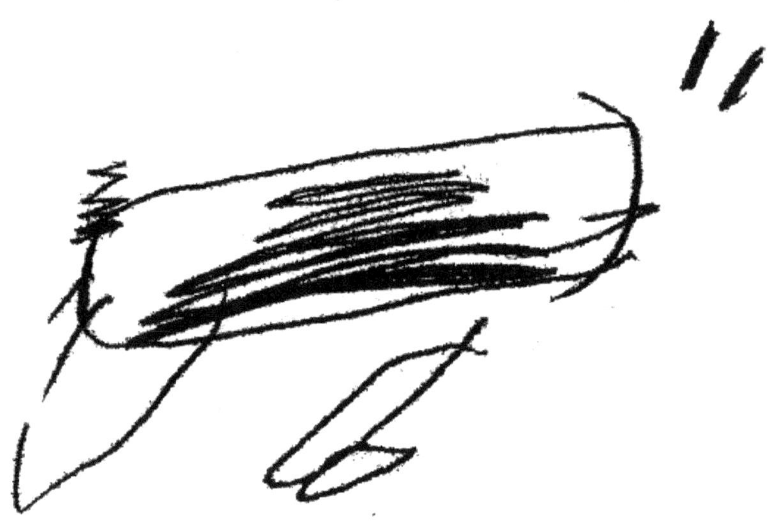

To be taken twice daily
Or sampled
It is in the name
It is safe
And
This is its length
So you can see how it floats
And it remains to be known
If it sinks too

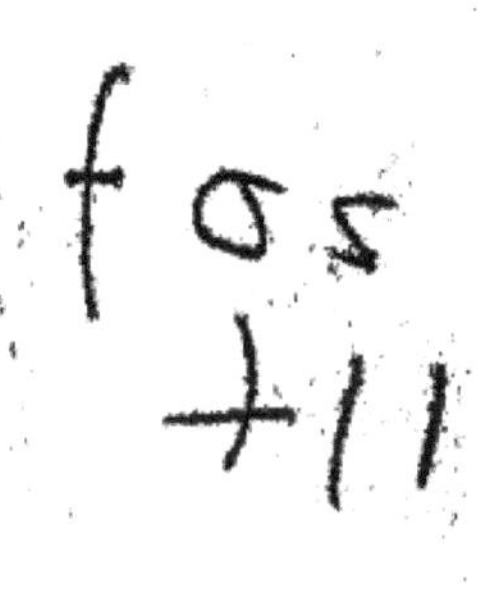

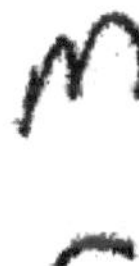

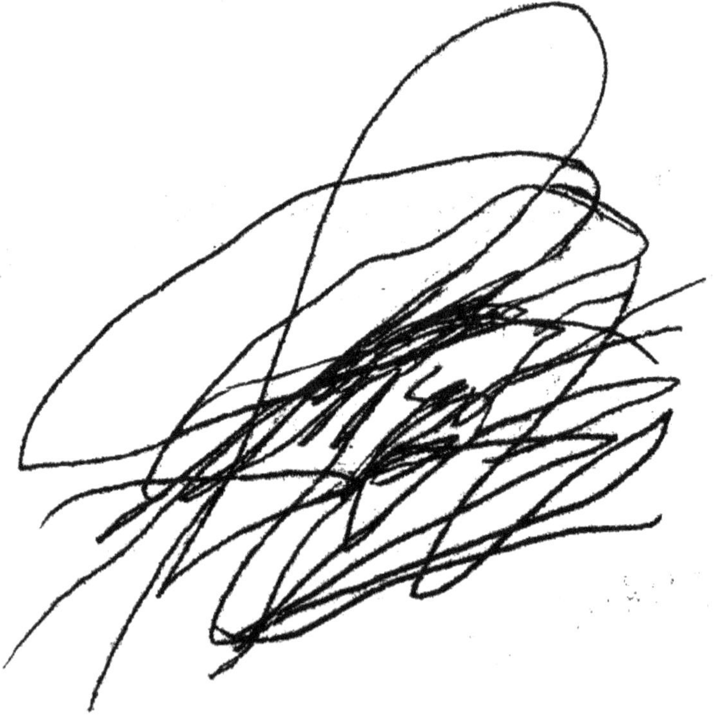

He scratched out his
Seeing the same way to
Is it about belonging?
It is about caring?
For the same way to be
well cared for
and placed and tagged and
numbered and
sampled and placed and placed
stop doubting and believe
Ro
Simple raft
It was the gravel that
Scratched the back of the hand
It was a name

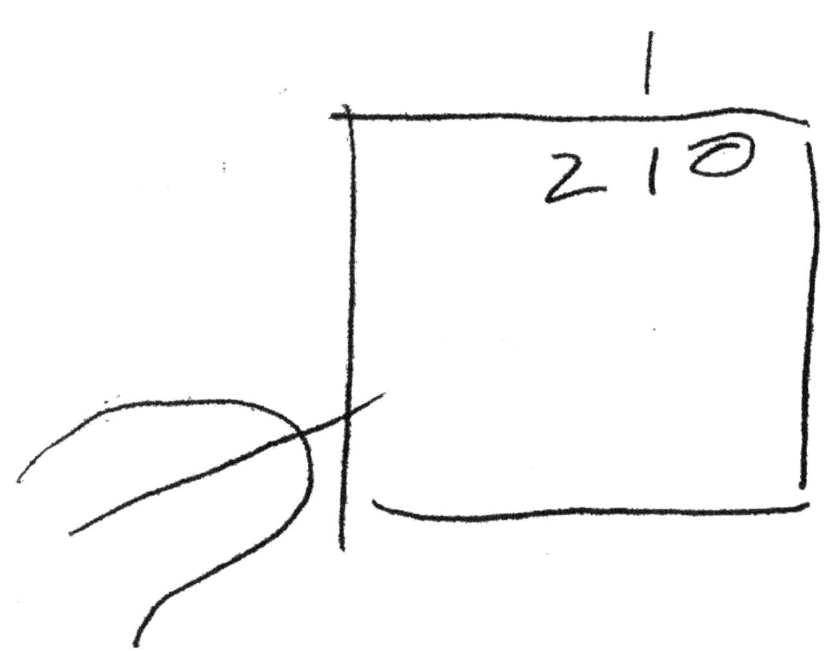
210

Half of globe and seeming to say
The travels were soft
And the cast was tight
To see the salt in the air was like
Licking the wound
The boxed
And delivery
And place
Where to seem the simple cash
To place the location and face t
And it was like a raft
You see that right?
You seem to say that
All time is like
Gravel scratches
And vinegar
Not fleshy wound but
Bound in a jacket
And cinched at the waist
And carefully cared for
And numb
To seem like the simple something
And a wave
And the air
And the empty place of a plot
And the geography of
Globe

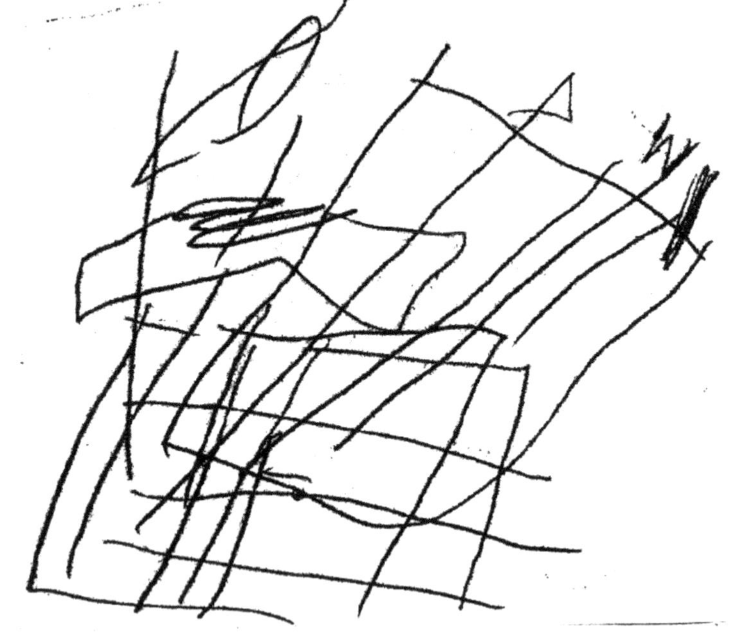

Or maybe a game
It was a toss of the
Rice and paste
The gambit
Or the which way to end
It isn't about the game
It is about the win
The weight of crown
And thistle
And wings sound
like the way I feel drowning
Can you crush the board
With finger you can form
And put your finger here
Check
It is
about the sound of the winning of the
weight
Afterwards
I know it isn't about crying

ke
lr
ded
wn
a
yt
te
d

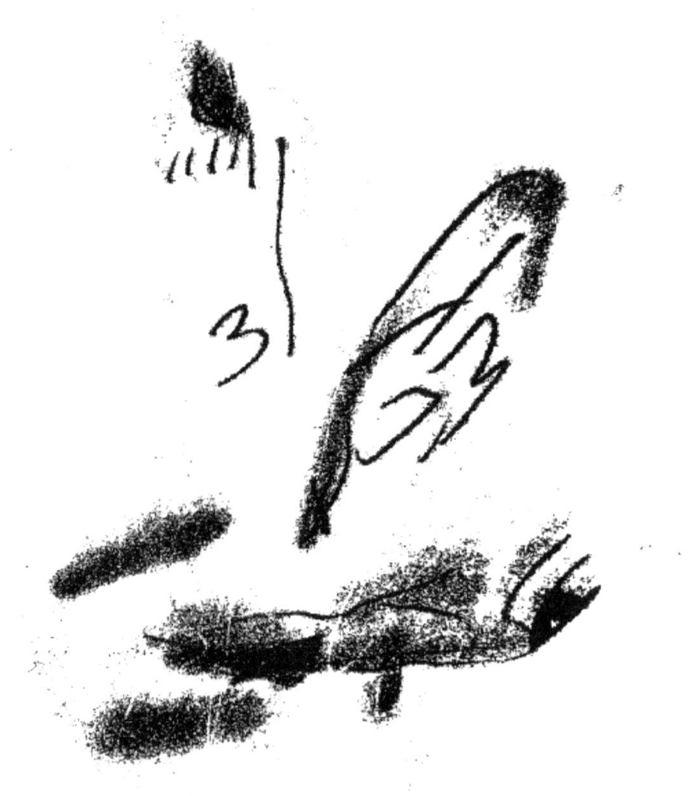

Residue
Smoke and filtered and fibered
And blood spinning
Crafted like its supposed to shape
You even numbered the ways you
Care to join the names
And its like a creation
And a memory of
Incense and
Did you light the
whole thing on fire for my sake?
There was a body on the raft

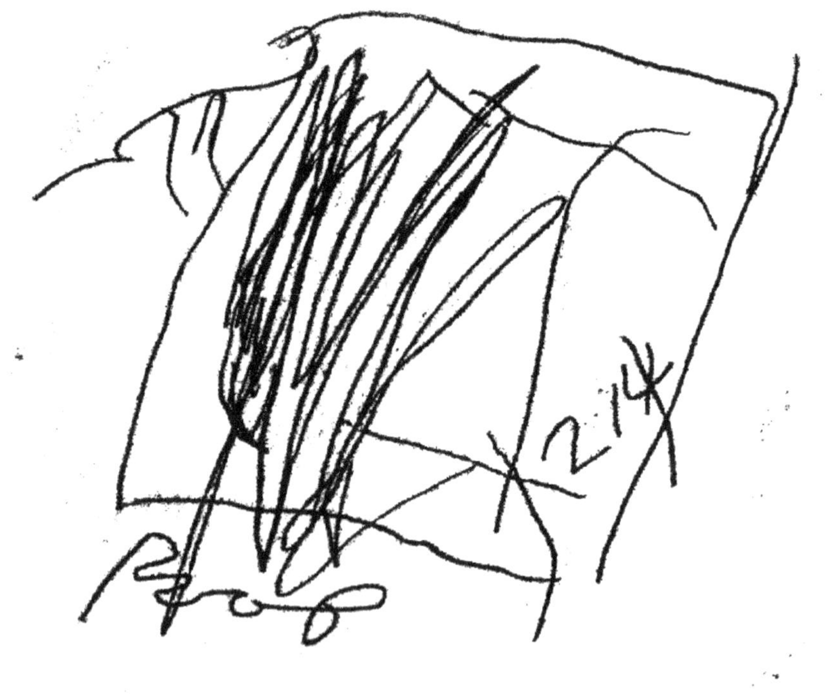

On the roof
It was a stain
Rust
Casual acquaintances
Followed by the crash of the window
The floor was simply the way to land
Maybe the pool
It was like a water
A raft
It was really about landing
You gave me
a location to land
but then it was like you
It was too dry for water
I will pass
And was it a meadow?
You keep it canceled
Like a folding chair
Like a way to stop caring
Or to stop
believing that it was the
right way to see
It is a day
Not long enough
Not the right length
Counting?
Why did it not matter enough?
It can't be about slippage

et
b
be
tt
/

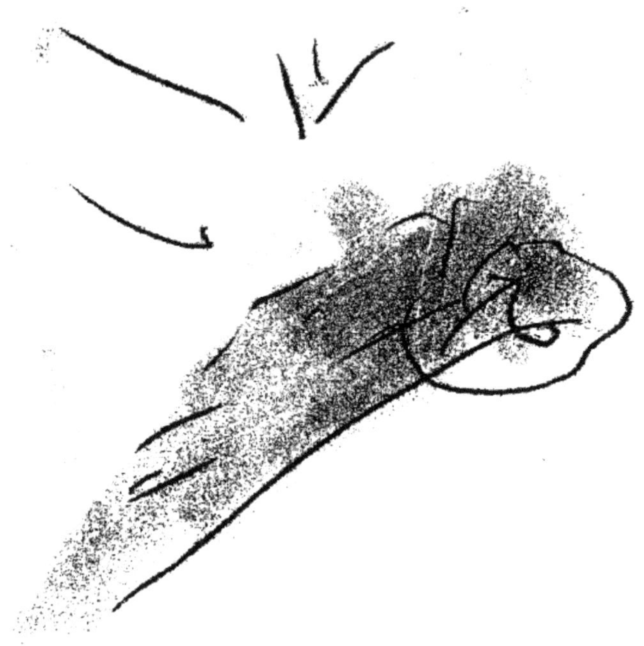

It was in the shallow end of the pool
You stepped in your name
In the mud
And the washed off way
It is about singing
About where to put your finger on it

nh
pst
md
ort
t
sr

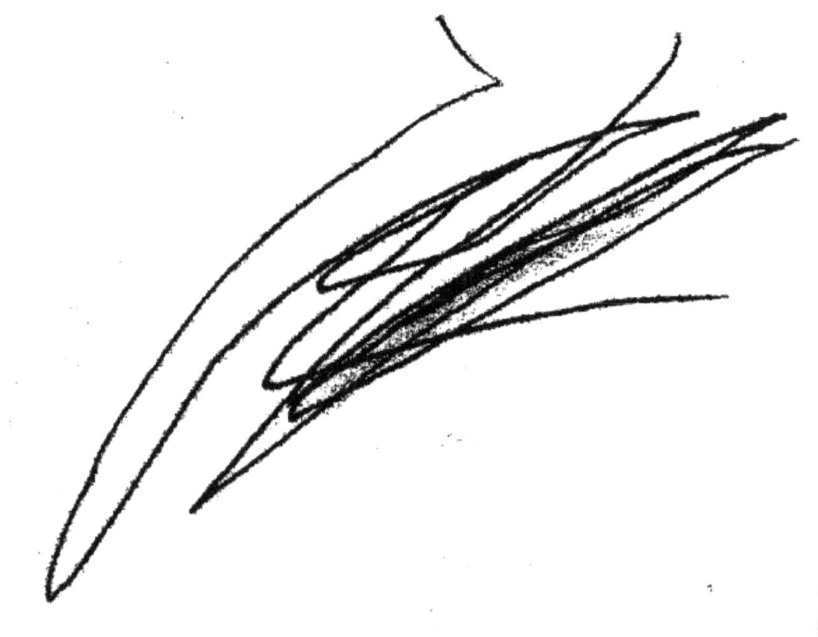

It sounded like a raven
But scratchy
Elongated like a boat
On a raft
The length was measured
To match a body
For my sake?
It is about indecision
Really
It is about
Shadows and the weight of stones
It isn't like dying

Sh
re
t
nw
nm

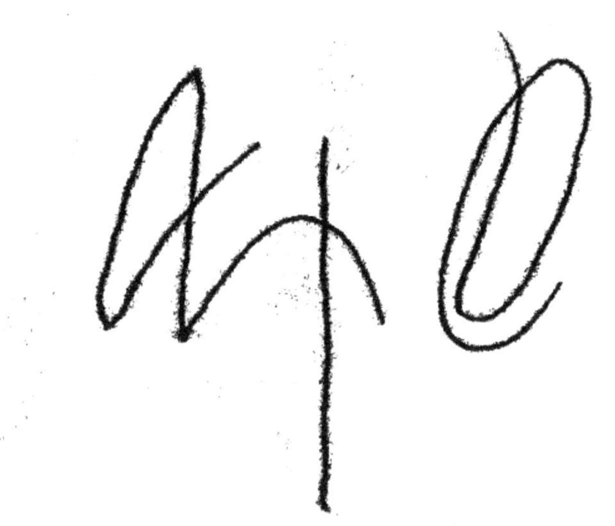

More like an age
An indication only
A signal for help
Or a
Find the back
It is a route
Paste the number on
the back of your hand
Like licking a stamp
Like licking salt in the wound
Your eyes light up when I say
It is like your name

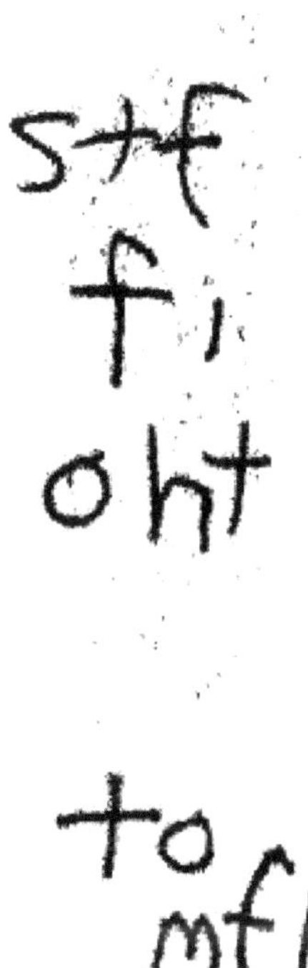

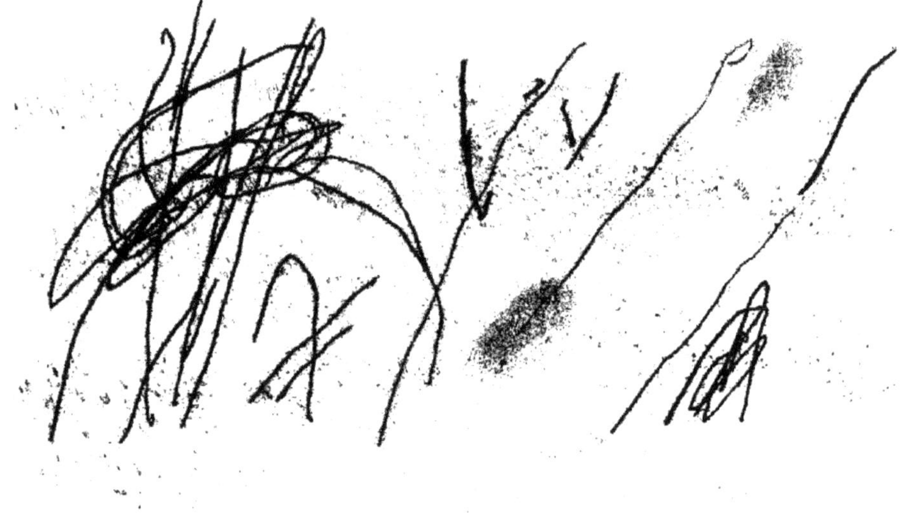

I have a feeling that you're
going to forget this
The way it is well
cared for and placed and tagged
and numbered
and sampled
and placed
and placed for it to
Rust
And dagger
It really became
about the way that the
gravel wrote your name on the
back of its hand
And singing
It was also place
And when it's the way
to sound a word
at the end of a breath
And the exhale
And when does
the word actually end
Is it the last part of the breath
Or the last part of the weight
Light it on fire for my sake
The whole thing

www.ingramcontent.com/pod-product-compliance
Lightning Source LLC
LaVergne TN
LVHW011051110826
845149LV00015B/3451

9781955498036